The Reed Handbook of Common
New Zealand
Ferns and
Fern Allies

The Reed Handbook of Common New Zealand Ferns and Fern Allies

Text by R.J. Chinnock
Illustrated by Eric Heath

REED

Published by Reed Books, a division of Reed Publishing (NZ) Ltd, 39 Rawene Rd, Birkenhead, Auckland. Associated companies, branches and representatives throughout the world.

ISBN 0 7900 0670 7

This edition designed by Jerry Rota

Printed in Singapore

Contents

Introduction

Ferns are common throughout New Zealand. They grow on the ground, along roads and tracks, on cliffs and banks, climb trees or sit perched on their branches. Even in the most inhospitable of places like windswept coastal cliffs or mountain tops, ferns can always be found either clinging to rocks, growing in rock crevices or growing under shrubs.

The ferns vary greatly in size from adder's tongue (pg 66) and *Azolla* (pg 13), which grow only a few centimetres long, to the mighty mamaku (pg 51), one of the true giants of the fern world, which may grow over 20 metres high.

The 59 ferns and fern allies brought together in this book represent about one-third of the total number found in New Zealand. They are 59 of the most common species which are most likely to be encountered on bush walks or in the forest. Some of these ferns like *Lygodium* (pg 69) are common in the particular parts of the country where they occur although they may be absent from other large areas.

For each species a description of the more important features is provided as an aid to identification. These, together with the illustrations, will make recognition of the common ferns and fern allies easy.

Fern classification

Ferns, like all plants and animals, have two names to enable any species to be referred to without difficulty. The first name places a plant into a group (genus), e.g. *Azolla, Grammitis, Lycopodium*; while the second name identifies the species from others in the genus, e.g. *L. fastigatum*, to distinguish it from other lycopodiums such as *L. scariosum* and *L. volubile*. The species of a genus may vary greatly in shape, size, mode of growth, type of leaves and the arrangement of the spore-bearing organs but they all share one or more features common to the genus.

   Plant names in books are often followed by the name of the person or persons who created them. The names of these people are often abbreviated.

Examples:

   (1) *Gleichenia dicarpa* R.Br. — Robert Brown (R.Br.) is the author of this species.

   (2) *Lastreopsis hispida* (Sw.) Tindale — Swartz (Sw.) originally described this species but placed it in another genus. Tindale transferred the species to the genus *Lastreopsis*.

In the filmy fern group (Plates 21–23) some classifications break them down into a large number of smaller genera so the alternative generic name has been provided in brackets.

   Common names have been added only where they are well known and in common usage, e.g. 'mamaku' or 'bracken'. Common names can often be misleading as a species may have more than one common name or a common name may cover a group of species, e.g. 'filmy fern'. There are 28 filmy ferns in New Zealand, so this name has little value.

   For each species the meaning of the specific name is also provided. The species name can be derived from the name of a person, as in 'billardierei', 'cunninghamii'; a location, as in 'novae-zelandiae', 'fluviatile', or from some feature of the plant, as in 'dicarpa', 'incisa', 'tenuifolia', 'filiforme' and so on.

Fern identification

Ferns and fern allies do not have flowers. Instead they produce spores on their leaves and reproduce by these. There are a number of basic terms which are used for ferns and fern allies and these are discussed below. In addition many of the terms are illustrated in figure 1.

The stem of the fern and fern allies is called the rhizome and this may creep along or under the ground, up the trunks of trees, or it may grow erect and may develop into a trunk. If the creeping rhizome grows rapidly then the leaves are scattered along it (*Microsorum, Hypolepis*), but if it grows slowly the fronds become clustered at the tip (*Grammitis, Asplenium*). Sometimes it is important to know whether the rhizome is covered in hairs or scales before a positive identification can be made.

The leaf of a fern is called a frond but in the fern allies other terms are applied because of their simple construction. The term leaf is used for them here.

The term frond consists of a stipe (stalk) and lamina (blade). The continuation of the stipe is called the midrib (rachis) and this may differ markedly from the stipe both in colour and covering of hairs and scales. The frond may be simple and undivided (*Grammitis billardierei*) or it may be divided into a number of basic divisions called pinnae. The pinnae may be arranged in opposite pairs or alternately along the midrib. If the pinnae are undivided then the frond is termed pinnate (*Blechnum fluviatile*, Plate 10). More commonly, however, the pinnae are further divided into secondary and tertiary pinnae so a frond in which the pinnae are divided into smaller, stalked pinnae is termed bipinnate and if those pinnae are again divided into yet smaller stalked pinnae it is termed tripinnate. The ultimate stalked segment is called the pinnule and this may be variously lobed or toothed.

The sporangia, the spore bearing capsules, their position and arrangement, and the structures associated with them, are very important for the identification of ferns and fern allies. If you take a mature fern frond and look on the underside you will see brown spots or lines in various positions. These spots or lines are the sori and if you take a closer look at a sorus with a 10x hand lens you will see that it is composed of numerous, small, round bodies which are the sporangia. Inside each sporangium are the fern spores and these are released when the sporangium dries and splits open. Very primitive ferns like

Asplenium have small sporangia, which are difficult to see unless you use a hand lens.

The sorus may be exposed on the undersurface of the frond or it may be variously covered by an indusium. The indusium varies greatly in shape and form, from small umbrella-like covers to reflexed portions of the pinnule margin as in *Adiantum* and *Pteris*.

The sporangia in the fern allies are very large. In *Lycopodium* the sporangia are produced singly at the base of the leaf. The spore-bearing leaves may occur in bands along the stem or they may be grouped together to form distinct structures called strobili.

In *Tmesipteris* the spore-bearing leaves are divided into two lobes, and two sporangia, which are fused together, sit in the notch at the base of the two lobes. The single structure formed by the two fused sporangia is called a synangium.

Hair and scale coverings of the rhizome and frond are very important for distinguishing species. The hairs may be simple, consisting of a single row of cells, or more complex with rounded glandular heads which make the fronds sticky (e.g., *Hypolepis rufobarbata*) or stellate hairs (e.g., *Pyrrosia eleagnifolia*).

Scales also vary considerably in shape, size and colour and they are of considerable importance. For example the two tree-fern genera can be distinguished by the presence or absence of scales. *Dicksonia* possesses only hairs while *Cyathea* has scales. By looking at the base of a frond one can tell which genus you have by the covering it has.

Variation in the frond size, its harshness and degree of hairiness largely depend on where the plant is growing. It is very important to keep this in mind when studying ferns. On coastal cliffs, for example, the mature fronds of *Microsorum pustulatum* may be as little as 5–6 cm long while in the forest they may be eight to ten times that size. The size of the fern frond should not be relied upon too greatly for identification. Instead, features of the sorus which are not greatly influenced by the environment and the general composition of the frond should be used. In general, species which are found under a wide range of habitats are the most variable.

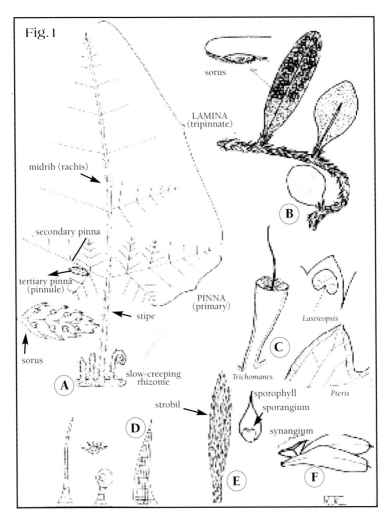

Fig. 1

sorus

LAMINA
(tripinnate)

midrib (rachis)

secondary pinna

tertiary pinna
(pinnule)

sorus

stipe

PINNA
(primary)

B

Lastreopsis

C

Trichomanes

Pteris

A

slow-creeping
rhizome

strobil

sporophyll

sporangium

synangium

D

E

F

A   A tripinnate frond of *Lastreopsis hispida* (diagrammatic) showing various
    important features of the frond structure.

B   *Pyrrosia eleagnifolia*, showing the long-creeping nature of the rhizome
    with scattered fronds.

C   Sorus coverings: *Trichomanes*, tubular indusium; *Lastreopsis*, kidney-
    shaped indusium; *Pteris*, modified reflexed margin of the pinnule.

D   Scale and hairs: a simple hair (left), stellate hair (above centre), glandlar hair
    (below centre), scale (right).

E   Strobilus of *Lycopodium* with one sporophyll removed to show the kid-
    ney-shaped sporangium at its base.

F   The bifid leaf of *Tmesipteris tannensis* with the bilobed synangium in the
    notch between the two lobes.

1

3

2

Adiantum, Pellaea, Azolla Plate 1
Maidenhair fern and others

1. *Adiantum cunninghamii* Hook.
   Common maidenhair fern
   Family: Adiantaceae
   (*cunninghamii*: named after A. Cunningham, a nineteenth-century botanist)

A small creeping fern with a black shining stripe which has brown scales towards the base. Lamina glabrous, consisting of 3–8 alternate pinnae. Pinnules oblong, distinctly stalked, their undersides whitish. Sori in the notches between the lobes, covered by a kidney-shaped indusium.

Common maidenhair fern is found throughout the country especially in drier situations on banks or in rock crevices along stream courses.

2. *Pellaea rotundifolia* (Forst.f.) Hook
   Family: Adiantaceae
   (*rotundifolia*: round leaved)

Rhizome slow-creeping, fronds linear, tufted together. Stripe and midrib covered with brown scales. Lamina pinnate, the pinnules rounded or oblong. Sori forming a continuous band along the margin but not reaching the base or apex.

This small fern is found throughout the country in drier open forests or amongst rocks in open places.

3. *Azolla filiculoides* Lam. Red azolla
   Family: Azollaceae
   (*rubra*: red)

Plants small, 1–2.5 cm long and broad, the leaves usually purplish-red (or green in shaded situations), triangular, overlapping like roof tiles. Roots undivided.

This small aquatic fern is common throughout the country on lakes, ponds and slow-moving rivers where it often forms a 'red bloom' over extensive areas. Reproduction is usually by fragmentation of the plant. This species also occurs in Australia and elsewhere. This species has previously been called *A. rubra* in New Zealand.

4

5

Pyrrosia and Anarthropteris

Plate 2

4. *Pyrrosia eleagnifolia* (Forst.f.) Ching
   Family: Polypodiaceae
   (*eleagnifolia:* leaves like Elaegnus, olive-like)

Rhizome long-creeping, much branched, covered in brown scales. Fronds variable in shape and size, 4–12 cm long, 1–2 cm broad, thick and fleshy, the upperside bright shiny green, the underside completely covered with pale brown, star-shaped hairs. Sori round, in rows on each side of the midrib, obscured by the dense hair covering.

   Pyrrosia is a sun-loving fern which occurs in various situations throughout the country from rocky coastal cliffs to the tops of trees. It is rarely seen in the forest unless a canopy tree has fallen where it clothes the upper branches. This fern may also be found on exotic trees or on stone walls. Until recently this species has been known as *Pyrrosia serpens*.

5. *Anarthropteris lanceolata* (J. Sm. ex Hook.f.) Pichi Serm.
   Family: Polypodiaceae
   (*lanceolata*: lance-shaped)

Rhizome short, scaly, emitting long woolly rootlets and producing new tufts of fronds at intervals. Fronds lanceolate, undivided, up to 25 cm long. Sori large, round, in a single row on each side of the midrib, unprotected.

   Anarthropteris lanceolata is usually found on the trunks of trees or on rocks and clay banks. It is common in lowland forests of the North Island, especially in Northland, and in the north and west of the South Island as far south as Greymouth.

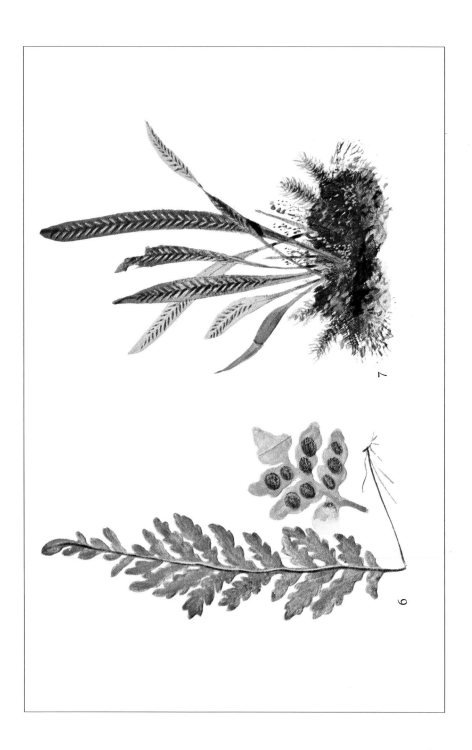

7

6

6. *Ctenopteris heterophylla* (Labill.) Tindale
    Family: Grammitidaceae
    (*heterophylla*: different leaved)

Rhizome short, scaly. Fronds 8–25 cm long, spreading or hanging, pinnatifid, with each segment usually toothed. Sori oblong to almost round, unprotected.

Very common throughout country in lowland to montane forest as an epiphyte or more rarely growing on rocks in open places. Also in Tasmania and Victoria.

This small species is very variable in its form. When growing on the trunks and branches of trees the fronds are pinnatifid but if found growing on rocks the plants become very small and the fronds are often undivided.

7. *Grammitis billardierei* Willd
    Family: Grammitidaceae
    (*billardieri*: named after J.J. Labilladière, an eighteenth/nineteenth-century botanist)

Rhizome short, slow-creeping, scaly. Fronds clustered, linear to linear-lanceolate, glabrous, to 15 cm long, the remnants of old fronds often persisting. Sori oblong, oblique to the midrib, often running together in older fronds and becoming indistinct.

A common little fern in lowland to montane forests throughout the country as an epiphyte on trees, fallen logs and mossy rocks. It also occurs extensively throughout south-eastern Australia and Tasmania.

8

Microsorum
Fragrant fern

Plate 4

8. *Microsorum scandens* (Forst.f.) Pichi Serm.
    Fragrant fern
    Family: Polypodiaceae
    (*scandens*: climbing)

Rhizome long-creeping, slender, scaly. Fronds pinnatifid or simple, pendulous, 10–35 cm long. Sori small, unprotected, in a single row each side of the midrib of the lobes. The sori are visible from the upper side of the frond by the raised circles which indicate their position.

Fragrant fern is common throughout the North Island and in the north and west of the South Island where it grows as an epiphyte on tree trunks and branches or on banks and mossy rocks. It is also common in south-eastern Australia.

Until recently this species has been known by the name *Phymatosorus scandens*.

9

9. *Microsorum pustulatum* (Willd.) Pic.Ser.
Family: Polypodiaceae
(*pustulum*: pustule, referring to spots on the fronds)

Rhizome long-creeping, thick and fleshy, green, partially covered with scales. Fronds pinnatifid or simple, often on the same piece of rhizome, thick and leathery, stiff, shiny, erect or hanging. Sori large, rounded, in a single row on each side of the midrib but closer to the margin. The position of the sori is visible on the upper side of the frond by raised spots. Fronds which do not produce sori usually have broader segments.

This fern is abundant throughout the country in all types of situations. It grows on coastal rocks where the fronds are small and frequently undivided, while in wet lowland to montane forests it creeps over the ground and up the trees and the fronds are usually pinnatifid and up to 60 cm long. This species also occurs in south-eastern Australia, Tasmania and Norfolk Island.

Until recently this species has been known by the name *Phymatosorus diversifolius*.

Asplenium
Spleenworts

Plate 6

10. *Asplenium bulbiferum* Forst.f.
    Hen & Chicken fern
    Family: Aspleniaceae
    (*bulbiferum*: bearing bulbils)

Rhizome short, erect, covered with scales. Fronds variable in size from 20–120 cm long, lanceolate, bipinnate to tripinnate, light green, thick and slightly fleshy. Pinnules variously dissected, with a few or numerous bulbils (small plants) growing on the upper side, sometimes absent. Sori oblong, covered by an indusium, but this is often obscured by the sporangia on very old fronds.

   Hen and chicken fern is found in forests and bush throughout the country where it is common on damp banks especially along streams. It also occurs in eastern Australia and Tasmania.

11. *Asplenium oblongifolium* Col.
    Shining spleenwort
    Family: Aspleniaceae
    (*oblongifolium*: oblong leaf)

Rhizome slow-creeping, densely covered with brown scales. Fronds pinnate, 20–100 cm long. Stipe brown, scaly towards the base. Pinnae oblong to lanceolate, bright shiny green above, dull green below, leathery, margins finely toothed. Sorus linear, covered with an indusium, but this often becomes obscure in old fronds.

   A common fern in forest situations throughout the country but less common in the South and Stewart Islands. May occur as an epiphyte or ground fern.

   Until recently this species was known as *Asplenium lucidum*.

12   13

Asplenium
Spleenworts

Plate 7

12. *Asplenium flaccidum* Forst.f.
Hanging spleenwort
Family: Aspleniaceae
(*flaccidum*: hanging down)

Rhizome slow-creeping with the fronds tufted together at the tip. Fronds 20–100 cm or more long, pale green, thick and leathery, flaccid. Pinnae entire, fluted, shallowly to deeply lobed. Sori linear, close to the margins, indusium present.

A common epiphytic fern in moist forests throughout the country. The fronds can often be seen hanging down out of clumps of epiphytic lilies (*Collospermum* species) which perch in the branches of trees. This species also occurs in eastern Australia and Tasmania.

13. *Asplenium polyodon* Forst.f.
Family: Aspleniaceae
(*polyodon*: many toothed, referring to the finely toothed margins of the pinnae)

Rhizome short, erect, scaly. Fronds bright dark green, tufted together, 20–100 cm long, the stipe and midrib scaly. Pinnae stalked, very oblique at the base, tapering to a long point, margins irregularly toothed. Sori numerous, oblique to midrib.

A common fern throughout the country except on the drier eastern side of the South Island. It usually occurs as an epiphyte on trees, especially in the organic accumulations at the bases of epiphytic lilies and on branches. Sometimes it grows on the floor of the forest on fallen logs and on mossy rocks. It also occurs in eastern Australia.

Until recently this species has been known by the name *Asplenium falcatum*.

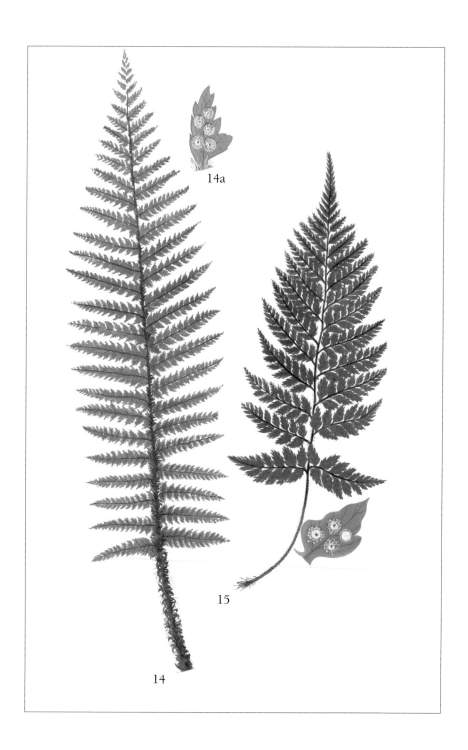

14a

15

14

Polystichum
Shield ferns

Plate 8

14. *Polystichum vestitum* (Forst.f.) Presl.
Prickly shield fern
Family: Dryopteridaceae
(*vestitum*: clothed)

Rhizome erect and eventually forming a small trunk, densely clothed in dark brown scales. Fronds 30–100 cm long, bipinnate, dark green, the stipe and midrib densely clothed in stiff brown scales. Pinnae stiff, prickly. Sori 4–8 per pinnule (14a). Indusium round, thin, the centre black.

   Prickly shield fern is a common to abundant fern in the cooler, wetter forests, especially in the South Island. In the North Island this species is more common at higher altitudes. After forests are cleared this species often covers hillsides.

15. *Polystichum richardii* (Hook.) J.Sm.
Family: Dryopteridaceae
(*richardii*: named after A. Richard, a nineteenth-century botanist)

Rhizome short, erect, covered with dark brown scales. Fronds 20–50 cm long in coastal forms but to over 100 cm long in inland forest forms. Stipe covered with dark brown scales and scurfy hairs. Lamina dark bluish-green above, light green below, firm and leathery or almost fleshy in some coastal forms, glabrous above but with scurfy hairs below. Sorus large, shield-like; sporangia black when mature.

   A common coastal fern in the North and South Islands. It is often found growing on coastal cliffs in crevices or under shrubs, and at the bases of coastal trees. Inland forms of this species grow much larger and are occasionally encountered in the forest on banks or on the forest floor.

17a

16a

16

17

Lastreopsis
Shield ferns

Plate 9

16. *Lastreopsis glabella* (A. Cunn.) Tindale
Family: Dryopteridaceae
(*glabella*: smooth)

A small fern with a short erect rhizome and a few tufted fronds at its tip. Fronds dull green, stipe smooth. Lamina glabrous except for the midrib and midribs of the pinnae, which are covered with fine, soft, reddish hairs, and the undersurface which has small appressed hairs. Sori small, at first covered with delicate pinkish, kidney-shaped indusia but these soon pushed to one side by the developing sporangia (16a).

This species is quite common in lowland forest throughout the country. It is frequently encountered along stream banks amongst rocks or on banks.

17. *Lastreopsis hispida* (Sw.) Tindale
Family: Dryopteridaceae
(*hispida*: with stiff hairs)

Rhizome slow-creeping, densely covered with stiff brown hairs. Fronds 30–100 cm long, stipe and midrib clothed with stiff brown hairs. Pinnae firm, finely dissected, midribs hairy. Sori 4–8 per pinnule (17a); indusium kidney-shaped.

Common in lowland forest as a ground fern or rarely as an epiphyte on the bases of trees and tree ferns. This species also occurs in Victoria and Tasmania. A very distinctive shield fern because of the stiff brown hairs on the stipe, midribs and rhizome.

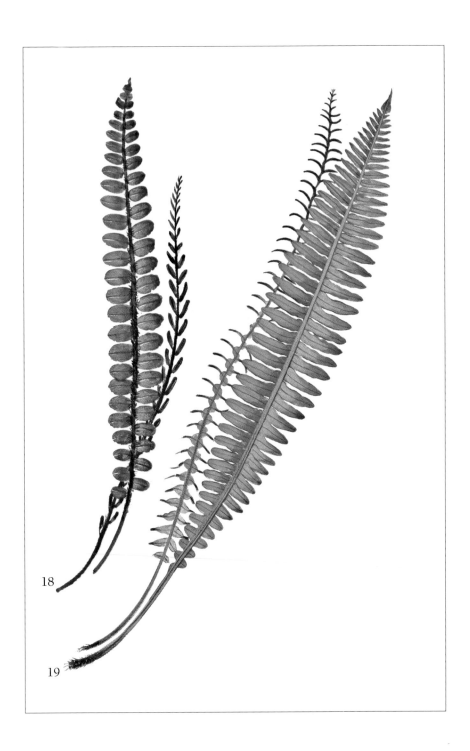

18

19

18. *Blechnum fluviatile* (R.Br.) Salom.
Family: Blechnaceae
(*fluviatile*: of or belonging to a stream)

Rhizome short, erect, scaly. Barren fronds spreading in a rosette and often lying on the ground, pinnate; the pinnae brownish-green, rounded to oblong. Fertile fronds erect and clustered together; the pinnae very narrow, erect, completely covered with sporangia on the underside.

   Common throughout the country especially from Rotorua southwards along the banks of streams. It is more common in the cooler mountain regions of the North Island. This species also occurs in south-eastern Australia and Tasmania.

19. *Blechnum discolor* (Forst.f.)
Keys Crown fern
Family: Blechnaceae
(*discolor*: of different colours)

Rhizome erect and eventually forming a small trunk. Fronds erect and spreading forming a crown. Barren fronds bright green above, whitish below. Fertile fronds erect, the segments narrow, brown; the lowermost pinnae with broad, sterile green bases.

   Common in forests throughout the country. In the North Island this species becomes more common at higher altitudes and is frequently the dominant ground cover.

21

20

32

20. *Blechnum procerum* (Forst.f.) Sw.
Family: Blechnaceae
(*procerum*: stretched out, long)

Rhizome long-creeping, branching, clothed with brown scales. Fronds pinnate, the barren ones bronze to deep green, erect or dropping, lanceolate-oblong, the margins finely toothed, the tip round or pointed; the fertile fronds brown, linear. The terminal pinna the longest, the lowermost pair the shortest.

A particularly common fern in forests, on forest margins or on banks in more open places throughout the country. In heavily browsed forests this species often becomes the most common ground plant.

21. *Blechnum novae-zelandiae* (L.) Schlecht.
Kio kio
Family: Blechnaceae
(*novae-zelandieae*: of New Zealand)

Rhizome long-creeping, branching, clothed with brown scales. Fronds pinnate, very variable in size, 20–360 cm long, usually hanging. Pinnae lanceolate, light green but often pink to red when developing, margins finely toothed, often wavy; the lowermost pinnae becoming small and round or similar in size to the middle pinnae.

This species is abundant throughout the country and is frequently seen clothing the cliffs and road-cuttings on most main roads. A very complex species which probably consists of a number of different species. Until recently this species was known as *Blechnum capense*.

34

22. *Blechnum chambersii* Tindale
Family: Blechnaceae
(*chambersii*: named after C. Chambers, a world authority on *Blechnum* ferns)

Rhizome short, erect, covered with dark brown scales. Fronds tufted at the tip, spreading, lanceolate, 15–60 cm long. Barren fronds pinnatifid, tapering to the base and tip, pinnae 2–5 cm long, deep green; fertile fronds erect, the pinnae linear, brown when mature.

   A common little forest fern which is usually found growing along the banks of streams or around waterfalls. This species also occurs in eastern Australia, South Australia and Tasmania.

23. *Blechnum filiforme* (A. Cunn.) Ettingsh.
Family: Blechnaceae
(*filiforme*: thread-like, referring to the fertile pinnae)

Rhizome long-creeping over the ground and up trees. Ground fronds small, never becoming fertile. Climbing fronds 20–50 cm long, hanging, the fertile fronds with very long, slender, drooping pinnae. Very common in forest throughout the country where it covers the ground and climbs up trees.

   This is one of our most remarkable species of *Blechnum*. It may creep over the forest floor for years to form dense carpets which never produce a fertile frond, but as soon as it starts climbing the trunk of a tree the fronds begin to enlarge and eventually it produces fertile ones.

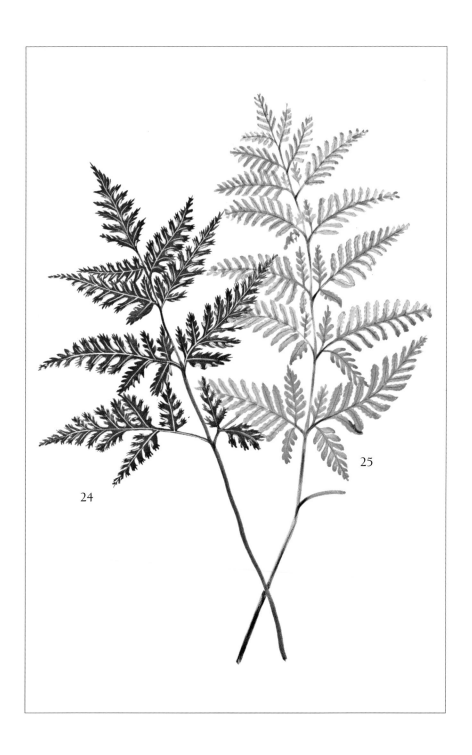

24

25

24. *Pteris macilenta* A. Rich.
    Family: Pteridaceae
    (*macilenta*: thin)

Rhizome short, erect, scaly. Fronds tripinnate, 30–100 cm long, spreading. Pinnae light green; pinnules triangular to lanceolate, lobed, the veins forming a net, prominent. Sori forming a continuous band along the margins in the lower part and protected by the modified margin of the pinnule.

   Common in drier lowland forests throughout the North Island and in the north and west of the South Island, as far south as Greymouth.

   This species is very variable and a number of varieties have been recognised. One of these, variety *saxatilis*, is often found amongst rocks in coastal forest or scrub, and has smaller triangular segments.

25. *Pteris tremula* R.Br.
    Family: Pteridaceae
    (*tremula*: trembling)

Rhizome short, erect, producing numerous fronds. Fronds tufted, erect but spreading, 30–150 cm long, pale green, soft, veins of pinnules free and not forming a network. Sori forming a continuous or broken band along the margin and protected by the modified pinnule margin.

   Common in drier forests in the North Island and in Marlborough, Nelson and Banks Peninsula in the South Island. This species is also widespread in Australia and on Norfolk Island.

26

27

Histiopteris and Hypolepis

Plate 14

26. *Histiopteris incisa* (Thunb.) J. Sm. Histiopteris
    Family: Dennstaedtiaceae
    (*incisa*: cut sharply and irregularly)

Rhizome creeping, thick, covered with flattened hairs. Fronds glabrous, broad lanceolate to lanceolate, 20–100 cm or more long, green to bluish-green, firm but soft; young uncoiling fronds milky bluish-green. Pinnae opposite or sub-opposite, pinnules of fertile fronds narrower than barren fronds. Sori forming a continuous band along the margins of the pinnules but not reaching the tip of the segments. Sori protected by the reflexed margin of the pinnule.

   An abundant fern throughout the country thriving in open situations such as along forest tracks, in clearings and forest margins, on hillsides and along streams. It often forms dense thickets along tracks and roads. In high country the old fronds die off in autumn and the new fronds start emerging from September onwards, depending on the altitude and frosts. This species is also common in Australia, Norfolk Island and elsewhere.

27. *Hypolepis ambigua* (A.Rich.) Brownsey and Chinnock
    Family: Dennstaedtiaceae
    (*ambigua*: ambiguous, doubtful, confusing)

Rhizomes long-creeping, much branched, densely covered with brown hairs. Fronds very variable, 20–100 cm or more long, lanceolate to deltoid, light to dark green, almost glabrous to very hairy. Lowermost pinnae obliquely angled to the midrib, the upper ones almost at right angles. Sori 2–8 per segment, circular, usually unprotected.

   Abundant throughout the country except in Northland. Usually found on the margins of forest, along forest tracks, in forest clearings or on open hillsides and on farmland. This species was previously known as *Hypolepis tenuifolia*.

28

Pteridium
Bracken

Plate 15

28. *Pteridium esculentum* (Forst.f.)
Nakai Bracken
Family: Dennstaedtiaceae
(*esculentum*: edible)

Rhizome long-creeping, black and fleshy, usually deeply buried. Fronds erect, tripinnate, very stiff, 50–200 cm long or sometimes as tall as 4 m when growing in shade on the margin of forest. During uncoiling of the fronds, the midrib rotates and this results in the lower pinnae pairs being projected in different directions. Pinnae firm and harsh, curved, green to brown, final segments linear. Sori form a band along the margins, covered by a delicate indusium which becomes obscured when the sporangia mature.

Over-abundant throughout the country, where it is found in every possible situation. This aggressive pioneer fern invades land after forest and scrub has been cleared for farming and soon becomes a nuisance. Bracken thrives only in full sun and soon vanishes once it is overtopped by shrubs and trees. This species is also widespread throughout temperate Australia, Norfolk Island and the Pacific.

30

29

29. *Paesia scaberula* (A. Rich.)
Kuhn Ring fern or hard fern
Family: Dennstaedtiaceae
(*scaberula*: rough)

Rhizome creeping, wiry, covered with brown hairs. Fronds 25–60 cm long, often drooping, sticky when young, rough when old. Midrib distinctly zig-zag, rough. Lamina green or yellow-green, tripinnate, covered with short, sticky hairs. Sori forming a band along margins of the pinnules but not reaching the base or tip, protected by the reflexed margin of the pinnule and a delicate inner indusium.

Abundant throughout the country on open, sunny hillsides and on the margins of forest where it often forms extensive patches. The fronds turn reddish-brown in autumn and gradually die off.

30. *Hypolepis rufobarbata* (Col.) Wakefield
Family: Dennstaedtiaceae
(*rufobarbata*: red bearded)

Rhizome long-creeping and much branched, densely clothed with reddish-brown hairs. Fronds lanceolate, 20–80 cm or more long, bipinnate to tripinnate. Stipe clothed with sticky, reddish-brown hairs of varying length. Pinnae soft, covered with reddish-brown, sticky hairs. Sori 1–6 per pinnule, orange-brown, unprotected and often completely covering the pinnule when old.

A common fern in forest throughout the country but becoming more common in the southern parts. This species is usually encountered on clay banks or in well lit situations such as forest clearings or along tracks. It can sometimes be found growing on fallen trees.

31a

31

Dicksonia
Tree-ferns

Plate 17

31. *Dicksonia fibrosa* Col.
Wheki-ponga
Family: Dicksoniaceae
(*fibrosa*: fibrous, referring to stem)

Trunk solitary, up to 7 m tall and to 50 cm diameter at the base, reddish-brown, soft due to the dense mat of fibrous roots which clothe the stem. Fronds numerous, dark green, spreading, the old fronds persistent, turning orange-brown, hanging down and forming a dense skirt. Stipe and midrib smooth, but covered with soft brown hairs when young. Sori numerous along the margins of the pinnules and protected by the modified margin of the pinnules and a semi-transparent indusium (31a).

Wheki-ponga extends from Auckland southwards but it is rare or absent from large areas. It is, however, particularly common in the Raetihi-Taumarunui region, where it occurs in forests and survives on cleared hillsides.

This tree-fern may be distinguished from the others by its massive reddish-brown trunk and the skirt of old fronds.

32

Dicksonia
Tree-ferns

Plate 18

32. *Dicksonia squarrosa* (Forst.f.) Sw.
Wheki
Family: Dicksoniaceae
(*squarrosa*: rough)

A small tree-fern with slender, solitary or clustered trunks. Trunk blackish-brown, very rough due to the persistent bases of fronds. Stipe and midrib very rough, almost prickly. Fronds small, rigid, very harsh, dark green but lighter on the underside. Sori numerous along the pinnule margins, large than but otherwise similar to Wheki-ponga.

Wheki is one of the most common tree-ferns. It is found throughout the country and thrives in swampy situations. The trunks are often used to construct walkways in swampy parts of forest tracks and it is not uncommon to find that the tips of cut-down trunks continue to grow and produce fronds. Unlike the other tree-ferns, wheki produces stolons which creep through the soil and produce new trunks resulting in groups of trunks.

Wheki is easily distinguished from the other tree-ferns by its slender, rough trunks which often occur in groups, and by the very harsh fronds which often form an orange-brown carpet on the forest floor.

33a

33b

33

33c

Cyathea
Tree-ferns

Plate 19

33. *Cyathea dealbata* (Forst.f.) Sw.
Ponga or silver fern
Family: Cyatheaceae
(*dealbata*: white-washed)

A robust tree-fern with a trunk 2–10 m tall. Stipe bases persistent, rough, covering the trunk. Fronds erect and spreading, the stipe 2–4 cm at base, covered with brown scales (33a and b — enlarged section). Lamina bright green above, white to light grey below. Sori large, brown, covered by a dome-shaped indusium.

Ponga is very common throughout the country, thriving in drier parts of forests especially on higher slopes, but also growing in more open situations in scrub and on exposed hillsides.

This species is easily distinguished by the whitish undersides of the fronds (33c — underside of secondary pinna). Very young plants which have not developed trunks may not exhibit the white bloom on the underside of the frond.

34b

34a

34

35a

35b

35

34. *Cyathea medullaris* (Forst.f.) Sw.
Mamaku or black tree-fern
Family: Cyatheaceae
(*medullaris*: marrow or pith)

A very robust tree-fern with trunks up to 20 m or more tall. Trunks black, with a distinctive hexagonal leaf-scar pattern, slender in the upper part but becoming thicker at the base due to the development of a dense mat of aerial roots. Fronds very large, the stipes black, the bases very thick and fleshy, covered with long black scales (34a). Lamina long and broad, the pinnae drooping at the tips. Sori numerous, large, dark brown, covered with a dome-like indusium (34b).

Mamaku is abundant throughout the country except in the drier eastern side of the South Island. It thrives in wet areas and is particularly conspicuous in valleys along streams.

35. *Cyathea smithii* Hook.f.
Family: Cyatheaceae
(*smithii*: after J. Smith, a nineteenth-century curator of Kew Gardens, England)

A small tree-fern with a trunk 3–8 m tall. Fronds small, narrow, bright green; the old stipe and midrib of the frond not drooping off but forming a skirt around the upper part of the trunk (35a). Sori numerous, small, partially covered by a scale-like indusium (35b).

Extending from Kaitaia southwards particularly in hilly forest valleys. In the North Island it is more common at higher altitudes.

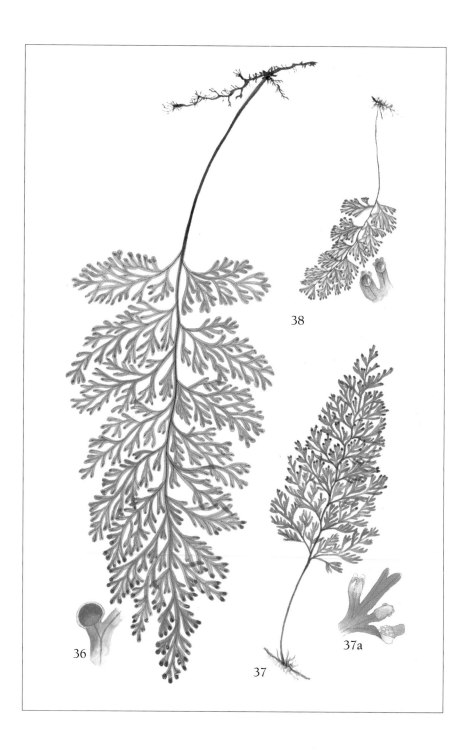

36

38

37

37a

Hymenophyllum
Filmy-ferns

Plate 21

36. *Hymenophyllum (Mecodium) dilatatum* (Forst.f.) Sw.
  Family: Hymenophyllaceae
  (*dilatatum*: spread out, referring to the very broadened segments)

Fronds 20–50 cm long, bright green; segments 2–3 mm broad. Stipe smooth, not winged. Sori large, terminating the segments.

  A common epiphyte on the living or fallen trunks of trees in forests throughout the country. Easily distinguished by its broad segments.

37. *Hymenophyllum (Mecodium) demissum* (Forst.f.) Sw.
  Family: Hymenophyllaceae
  (*demissum*: let down, referring to the drooping fronds)

Fronds 15–30 cm long, scattered along a wiry, creeping rhizome. Stipe smooth, narrowly winged, the wing green, straight or wavy. Lamina deep green; sori at the ends of the segments, usually in pairs (37a).

  Abundant throughout the country especially in lowland forest where it frequently carpets the forest floor. It also grows on the lower parts of trees and tree-ferns.

38. *Hymenophyllum (Mecodium) flabellatum* Labill.
  Family: Hymenophyllaceae
  (*flabellatum*: fan-shaped)

Rhizome and stipe at first covered with brown, woolly hairs but eventually glabrous. Fronds 4–25 cm long, light green, pinnae fan-shaped. Sori small, at the ends of segments.

  A small filmy fern which is widespread throughout the country. It is commonly found covering the trunks of trees and tree-ferns but occasionally grows on damp banks. When growing on tree-ferns the fronds are very small and triangular. This species also occurs in eastern Australia.

39

40

41

41a

Hymenophyllum
Filmy ferns

Plate 22

39. *Hymenophyllum (Mecodium) scabrum* A. Rich.
Family: Hymenophyllaceae
(*scabrum*: scabrid, rough)

Fronds up to 60 cm long, dark green to brownish-green, segments entire. Stipe covered with stiff, brown hairs; midriff hairy. Sori at the tips of segments.

A common filmy fern encountered on the living and fallen trunks of trees in forests throughout the country.

40. *Hymenophyllum (Mecodium) multifidum* (Forst.f.) Sw.
Family: Hymenophyllaceae
(*multifidum*: many divisions)

Fronds bright to deep green, 2–30 cm long, curved or straight. Pinnae segments finely toothed. Sori large, oblong and distinctly two-valved, restricted to the upper part of the frond towards the bases of the segments near the midrib. Valves up to 3 mm long, often with a bristle projecting out of the sorus.

Abundant throughout the country at all altitudes as an epiphyte on tree trunks, on mossy rocks, on the ground under scrub, in the forest or in rock crevices in exposed mountain situations.

41. *Hymenophyllum revolutum* Col.
Family: Hymenophyllaceae
(*revolutum*: rolled back)

Fronds small, 3–10 cm long. Stipe thin and bristle-like; midrib smooth, not winged. Pinnae segments coarsely toothed. Sori on short lateral segments, very large, two-valved, the valves toothed (41a).

A common little filmy fern found on the trunks of trees and on fallen logs in forests throughout the country.

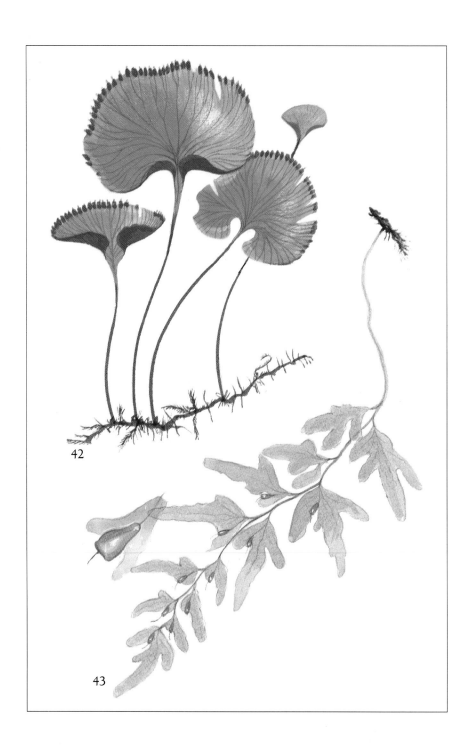

42

43

Trichomans
Filmy ferns

Plate 23

42. *Trichomanes (Cardiomanes) reniforme* Forst.f.
Kidney fern
Family: Hymenophyllaceae
(*reniforme*: kidney-shaped)

Rhizome tough and wiry, long-creeping. Stipe wiry, brown, glabrous. Lamina deep green, leathery, kidney-shaped. Sori numerous, in a dense band along the margin, cup-shaped, embedded in the lamina, the sporangia exserted on a common stalk.

Common throughout the country except for the eastern part of the South Island. Kidney fern forms extensive mats on rocks, banks and the forest floor. More rarely it is found growing on the trunks of trees. One of our most well known ferns, it is easily distinguished by its kidney-shaped fronds.

43. *Trichomanes (Polyphlebium) venosum* R.Br.
Veined bristle-fern
Family: Hymenophyllaceae
(*venosum*: conspicuously veined)

Fronds 2–8 cm long, light green, translucent, pendulous. Pinnae and stipe glabrous; veins of segments conspicuous. Sori immersed in the lobes of segments close to the midrib. A bristle up to 10 mm long may develop from the sorus.

A small filmy fern which is common throughout the country especially on the trunks of tree-ferns. This species also occurs in eastern Australia and Tasmania.

45a

45

44

Pneumatopteris and Lindsaea

Plate 24

44. *Pneumatopteris pennigera* (Forst.f.) Holttum
    Family: Thelypteridaceae
    (*penniger*: feather)

Rhizome short, erect, and sometimes forming a short trunk to 50 cm. Fronds 30–150 cm long, spreading. Stipe dark brown, thick and slightly fleshy at the base, scaly in the lower part. Pinnae bright green, thin, deeply lobed, veins prominent. Sori numerous, jet black when mature, brown when old, unprotected.

Abundant in forests throughout the country at lower altitudes. It thrives on rich alluvial soils in forest valleys and is particularly conspicuous along stream banks, where it attains its greatest size.

45. *Lindsaea trichomanoides* Dryand.
    Family: Lindsaeaceae
    (*trichomanoides*: like *Trichomanes*)

A small fern with a slow-creeping rhizome. Fronds clustered, 8–30 cm long. Stipe slender, wiry, reddish-brown, glabrous. Lamina pinnate, bipinnate to sub-tripinnate, lanceolate; pinnae segments thick, firm, variously dissected. Sori form a continuous band around the apex of the segment, protected by a delicate indusium which opens out towards the margin (45a).

Common in the North Island, especially in the northern part; rare and local in the South Island. This is a particularly common species on drier slopes in beech (*Nothofagus*) and kauri (*Agathis*) forest.

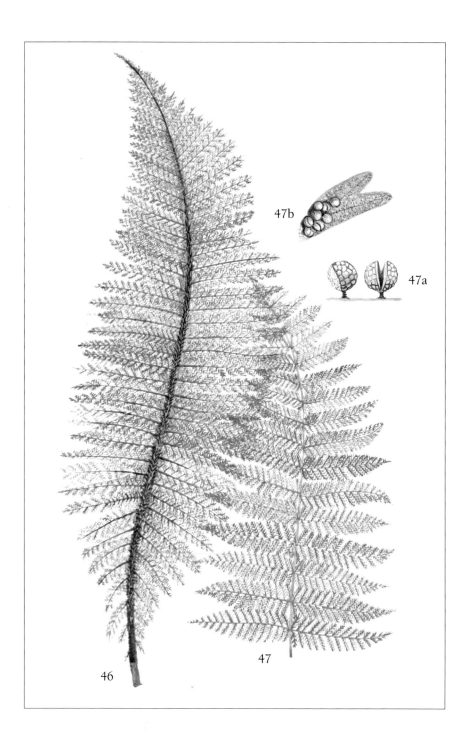

47b

47a

46

47

Leptopteris
Crape fern

Plate 25

46. *Leptopteris superba* (Col.) Presl.
Crape fern, Heruheru, Prince of Wales feather
Family: Osmundaceae
(*superba*: superb, magnificent)

Rhizome erect, eventually forming a trunk to 1 m tall. Fronds 20–100 cm or more long, rich deep green, lanceolate, clustered, spreading and forming a crown. Pinnae feathery, very finely dissected, the pinnule segments overlapping giving the frond a crape-like feel. Sporangia very large and visible with the naked eye, scattered along the midribs of the pinnules.

This fern only thrives in cool, wet forest. It is rare from the Auckland district northwards, but becomes more common from Rotorua southwards, and it is in the cool high rainfall areas of Westland that it attains its largest size. In the North Island it is usually found at higher altitudes.

47. *Leptopteris hymenophylloides* A. Rich.
Heruheru
Family: Osmundaceae
(*hymenophylloides*: like *Hymenophyllum*)

Rhizome erect and sometimes forming a small trunk. Fronds few, clustered, to 90 cm long. Stipe green to brown, winged at the base. Lamina pale green, translucent, finely dissected; the pinnule segments flat and not overlapping. Sporangia large (47a), similar to *L. superba*, scattered on the midribs in the lower part of the pinnae (47b).

This species is much more common than crape fern because of its tolerance of drier situations. It is widespread throughout the country, particularly on banks of streams. Young plants of this species are easily mistaken for a filmy fern.

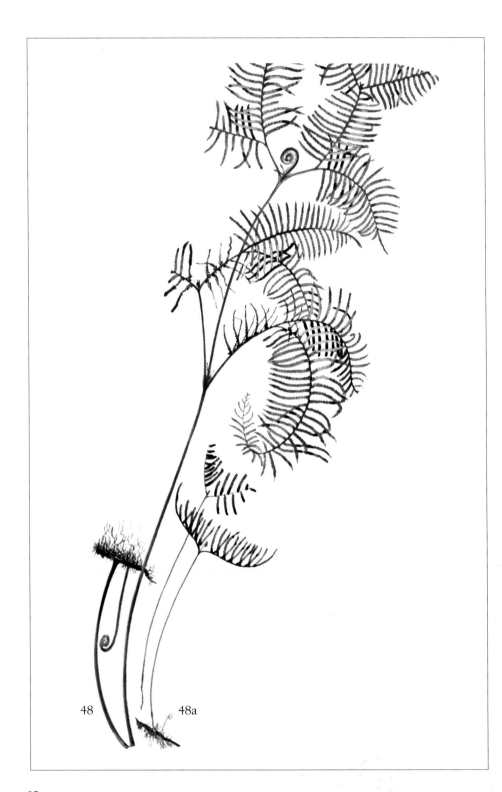

48   48a

Gleichenia
Swamp umbrella fern

Plate 26

48. *Gleichenia dicarpa* R.Br.
Swamp umbrella fern
Family: Gleicheniaceae
(*dicarpa*: two fruited)

Rhizome long-creeping, slender, wiry, much branched, covered with scales. Fronds very variable, 20–100 cm or more long, consisting of 1–3 tiers of opposite pinnae. Pinnae forked 2–3 times, the midribs clothed in brown scales and hairs. Ultimate segments small, 2–3 mm long, rounded, pouched on the underside. Sporangia brown, 1–2 per segment.

A common fern found throughout the country in open scrublands and swampy situations. The tip of each frond has a dormant bud which may develop over a period of time to produce new pairs of pinnae. As a result the lower pinnae pairs may be dead and disintegrated while new pinnae are open at the top.

This species often forms dense thickets with the pinnae interlacing or growing up through shrubs. *Gleichenia dicarpa* var. *alpina* (48a) is restricted to mountain swamps (except in the south of the South Island) and forms extensive low cushions. This species also occurs in eastern Australia and Tasmania.

49a

49

Sticherus
Umbrella fern

Plate 27

49. *Sticherus cunninghamii* (Hook.) Ching
Umbrella fern
Family: Gleicheniaceae
(*cunninghamii*: named after A. Cunningham, a nineteenth-century botanist)

Rhizome creeping, much branched, densely clothed with dark brown scales. Stipe 10–20 cm long, scaly at first. Lamina bright green above, whitish below, divided into two halves which fan out to form an umbrella. A dormant bud occurs in the notch between the two halves and this sometimes develops and produces 1 or 2 more pinnae. Sori in rows on the undersides of the ultimate segments, unprotected (49a).

Common throughout the North Island particularly at higher altitudes. It is particularly common on banks throughout the central volcanic area. In the South Island it is rare and local. Ground forms of this species frequently develop the second and third pairs of pinnae while the more typical form (illustrated) grows on steep banks.

65

50

51

52

51a

Ophioglossum and Schizaea
Adder's tongue and comb ferns

Plate 28

50. *Ophioglossum coriaceum* A. Cunn.
Adder's tongue
Family: Ophioglossaceae
(*coriaceum*: tough, leathery)

Rhizome small, fleshy, with buds developing on the roots to produce new tufts of fronds at intervals. Sterile fronds fleshy, bright green, lanceolate, 1–8 cm long. Fertile spike projected above the sterile frond on a fleshy stalk. Sporangia in two rows embedded in the spike.

Widespread throughout the country but rarely seen because of its small size and un-fernlike appearance. This species grows in open grassland, around lakes and tarns, open river flats and in scrubland.

51. *Schizaea fistulosa* Labill.
Comb fern
Family: Schizaeaceae
(*fistulosa*: hollow and cylindrical)

Rhizome slow-creeping, covered with glossy brown hairs. Fronds clustered; stipe grass-like, 8–40 cm long, smooth, usually terminated by a comb-like fertile lamina 1–3 cm long, brown at maturity. Sporangia covering the pinnae but obscured by the folding together of the two halves of the lamina.

Quite common from North cape to East Cape on clay or poorly drained soils, usually in manuka scrub. South of East Cape it is rare and local but extends as far as Stewart Island.

Schizaea fistulosa var. *australis* (51a) is common in swamps and rarely exceeds 10 cm high.

52. *Schizaea bifida* Willd.
Family: Schizaeaceae
(*bifida*: divided into two)

Fronds few, clustered; stipe 6–30 cm long, simple or branched once or twice, rough to feel. Fertile lamina pale brown, short and broad, 1–2 cm long, 6–8 mm broad.

Found in the same situations as *Schizaea fistulosa* in the North Island but restricted to pakahi soils near Takaka and Collingwood in the South Island.

53b

53

53a

Lygodium
Mangemange

Plate 29

53. *Lygodium articulatum* A. Rich.
Mangemange
Family: Lygodiaceae
(*articulatum*: jointed)

Rhizome long-creeping, covered with brown scales. Ground fronds (53a) divided into two pinnae which are forked 2–4 times, pinnules up to 10 cm long. Climbing fronds of 'unlimited growth' climbing over scrub and up trees 10–20 m or more. Sterile pinnae twice branched, green to yellow-green. Fertile pinnae branched many times; pinnules small, deeply lobed with 8–12 sporangia per lobe (53b).

Mangemange is abundant in forests throughout the northern North Island to just south of Rotorua. It often forms dense thickets made up of the numerous twining midribs.

54

55

Fern Allies

Huperzia and Lycopodium

Plate 30

The Lycopods are a group of fern allies with small, spirally arranged, simple leaves which are scale- or strap-like. Fertile leaves are grouped together in bands along the stem or in cone-like heads called strobili. A single, yellow, kidney-shaped sporangium occurs at the base of each leaf.

54. *Huperzia varia* Spring
Family: Lycopodiaceae
(*varia*: variable)

Stems pendulous from trees, clustered to form clumps, branched many times. Leaves arranged in a spiral, linear, spreading to 1 cm long. Spore-bearing leaves small, 1–2 mm long, at the tips of branches.

A common epiphyte in forests throughout the country and frequently seen hanging from the bases of epiphytic lilies (*Collospermum*). Occasionally this species grows on the ground at higher altitudes and in such forms the stems grow erect. Until recently this species was known as *Lycopodium billardieri*.

55. *Lycopodium fastigiatum* R.Br.
Family: Lycopodiaceae
(*fastigiatum*: clustered and erect)

Rhizome creeping and producing erect, branched stems. Leaves small, spirally arranged, green to bright orange, 3–5 mm long. Spore-bearing leaves aggregated together into a strobilus, the strobili grouped together at the tips of branches.

Very common in scrublands to montane grasslands throughout the country, more common at higher altitudes in the North Island. In exposed mountain situations the stems become prostrate and commonly turn bright orange. This species also occurs in eastern Australia and Tasmania.

57a

57

57b

56a

56

Lycopods

Plate 31

56. *Lycopodium scariosum* Forst.f.
    Family: Lycopodiaceae
    (*scariosum*: thin, dry and membranous, not green)

Rhizome creeping, yellowish. Stems much branched, flattened, the leaves of two forms; the upper ones flattened into one plane and the lower ones in a row and overlapping (56a). Spore-bearing leaves grouped together to form a strobilus, the strobili raised on stalks at the tips of branches, solitary or paired.

    A common species in mountain regions from Rotorua southwards. This species also occurs in Victoria and Tasmania.

57. *Lycopodium volubile* Forst.f.
    Family: Lycopodiaceae
    (*volubile*: twining)

Main stems climbing and twining around branches of shrubs or crawling over banks or on the ground. Leaves of two types: the lateral ones flattened into one plane and the upper ones small, scale-like and appressed to the midrib (57a). Strobili numerous, grouped together on branches in very large numbers. Sporophylls ovate, sporangia kidney-shaped (57b).

    A common lycopod throughout the country in scrubland, on the margins of forest, along forest tracks and on banks and road cuttings. Plants in exposed situations sometimes turn yellow to orange.

59

58

Psilopsids Plate 32

This small group of fern allies do not have roots but merely an underground rhizome which produces aerial stems. *Tmesipteris* has leaves arranged in a spiral or flattened into one plane and spore-bearing leaves which are divided into two, with two fused sporangia (called a synangium) in the notch between the two divisions of the leaf.

58. *Tmesipteris elongata* Dang
 Family: Psilotaceae
 (*elongata*: elongate, stretched)

Aerial stems undivided or divided 2–3 times in the upper part, 10–80 cm or more long, pendulous. Leaves 1–4 cm long, dull green on both surfaces, flexible. Synangia elongate, rounded at the ends, dropping off when old.
 A common epiphyte on the trunks of tree-ferns in the North Island and in the north and west of the South Island. This species also occurs in Victoria and Tasmania.

59. *Tmesipteris tannensis* (Spreng.) Bernh.
 Family: Psilotaceae
 (*tannensis*: named after Tanna Island, New Hebrides, where it was
 thought that this species had been collected)

Aerial stems unbranched, pendulous, 10–80 cm or more long. Leaves dark green, shiny on one surface, 0.5–3 cm long. Synangium pointed at both ends, the two halves angled to each other.
 This species is abundant throughout the country as an epiphyte on the trunks of trees and tree-ferns, on organic accumulations on banks and at the bases of trees.